Counter-Print Packaging

A modern compendium of graphic design
for packaging

COUNTER-PRINT

Also from Counter-Print
Robert Samuel Hanson
Animal Logo
Monogram Logo
Human Logo
Alphabet Logo
Nature Logo
Abstract Logo
Modern Heraldry
Icon
From Japan
From Scandinavia
Book Cover Design from East Asia
Art Marks
Cruz Novillo: Logos
Logos From Japan

COUNTER-PRINT PACKAGING

Published by Counter-Print
counter-print.co.uk
Designed by
Jon Dowling & Céline Leterme
ISBN No.
978-0-9935812-5-0
First Published in 2018
©Counter-Print

Contents

With special thanks to all the contributors for their support, time and talent.

Foreword

Early humans would have used packaging to store and transport food and artefacts as nomadic hunters and gatherers, even before the concept of trade. The history of packaging is, in other words, as old as the history of humankind and predates commerce. The earliest examples of man's artifice to meet the needs of survival would include the natural materials available at the time: baskets of reeds, wineskins, wooden boxes, pottery vases, wooden barrels, woven bags and so on.

Much later, as technology advanced, so too did packaging materials and processes. Today, packaging is one of the most influential and widespread forms of communication with consumers, as it provides a firsthand customer touchpoint for brands and, due to the numerous and varied quantities of consumer-based products that are produced in modern society, has one of the widest ranges of applications of all the forms of graphic design.

The millions of different products on sale today require unique and individual packaging to set them apart from the competition when they reach their retail destinations. The packaging is also burdened with the mission of showing off, or identifying the contents, making them attractive and enticing to the prospective customer.

The art of packaging – the care taken with its conception, the concealment, the expectancy of the consumer – has always delighted me. I appreciate the thought that has gone into it's application and I cheerfully open packages with a certain air of expectancy. As with a well wrapped gift, we feel grateful when we receive a package which directly conveys from the sender, not just their wish to send it without damaging the contents, but a sense of care or even love.

Our first impression is formed by the packaging. It helps in our understanding of the contents and the company that has made it. Done well, packaging is capable of providing visceral clues designed to affect the consumer's perception. It can encourage potential buyers to purchase a product and it can reflect the brand's message and identity. It is deceptively simple and very hard to pull off.

Once we as consumers are triggered to make the purchase, the product is taken home and unwrapped and the packaging often discarded. This is the ephemeral nature of much modern packaging, it's life is finite and, however beautifully it is designed, it is often destined to be thrown away.

In the UK alone we produce more than 170m tonnes of waste every year, much of it food packaging. While packaging has revolutionised the way we store and consume food, there is now so much of it that landfills can't cope and, as such, the need for designers to act in an environmentally responsible way has never been more important.

The current generation of designers is more attuned than ever to the need for environmental awareness. There is a general public concern, with regard to both limited resources and the safe disposal of packaging waste. A look at contemporary packaging, as seen in this book, suggests that, as well as new printing processes and the discovery of new materials, a preservation of our natural resources and a concern for the impact of this output have come to the fore – whether this be through the use of bio-packaging for sandwiches and water-soluble paper, or trends in minimal packaging and so on.

Of course, some of the packaging shown in this book is so beautiful, tactile and well crafted that it can have serious expectations of a second life after it's primary purpose has been achieved. I have a beautifully designed box from Kiehl's as proof of this, which now serves as a treasure chest for my own most precious things. Good packaging design can have a very personal relationship with it's owner, which is why it makes such a strong conduit for a brand's message. When done well, it enhances the overall brand story, engaging, informing and ultimately leaving us with a sense of the brand's ethos.

Jon Dowling
Counter-Print

counter-print.co.uk

"Our first impression is formed by the packaging. It helps our understanding of the contents and the company that has made it."

Counter-Print

Food

"They started as an 'American Burger' restaurant and we ended up positioning them as a 'Kiwi' lifestyle brand advocating for people to smash life, live it to the full and not be afraid of doing whatever they are passionate about."

Pop & Pac

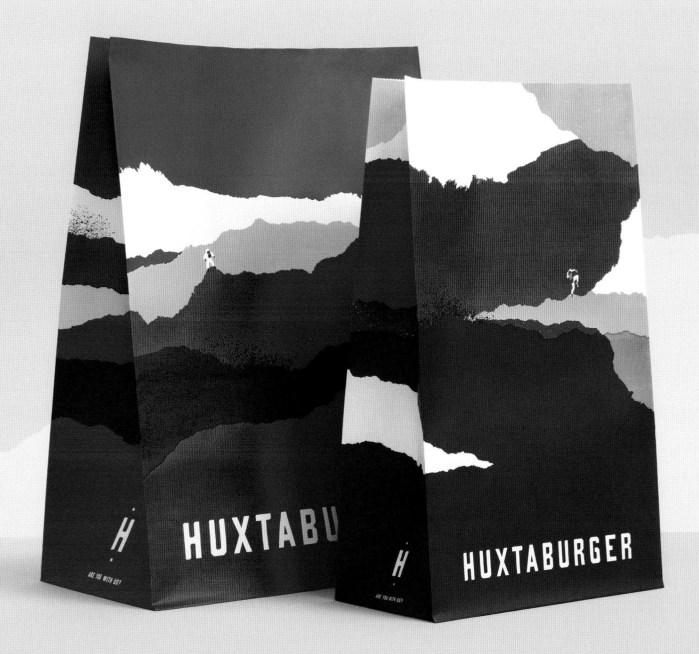

Huxtaburger

~~~~~~

Pop & Pac
pop-pac.com

What was the brief for this project and how did the opportunity come about?
The project actually came about as a referral from a company we use to produce/print most of our packaging projects. The brief was initially for a brand refresh, however, after our initial workshop, it was clear that we needed to take Huxtaburger in a new direction. They started as an 'American Burger' restaurant and we ended up positioning them as a 'Kiwi' lifestyle brand advocating for people to smash life, live it to the full and not be afraid of doing whatever they are passionate about; whether it's eating a big fat juicy burger or base jumping off a cliff.

Can you talk us through the design process?

We started with a tailored design questionnaire that on the surface poses a lot of seemingly abstract questions, however they are all targeted in a way that get the client thinking less literally and more laterally. This process helps us lock in a brand story and helps with establishing our creative territories, it also integrates the client in the creative process and solidifies the collaborative process.

Once we are through this first stage, the thoughts that come out of this process then form the starting points for our ideas and creative directions. These ideas are first presented to the client in the form of 'design territory' moodboards. The client choses one creative territory, of which we develop three concepts. Once one concept is chosen, we refine and apply the visual elements (logos, patterns, language, type etc) to all the applications, from packaging and web to signage and more.

How did you develop the illustration/ graphic style?

The creative response took inspiration from the 'urban' landscape (of the restaurants) and 'flavour' landscape (of the burgers). The textures of different ingredients and the various locations of the Huxtaburger stores all informed the textures in the packaging. The logo was a nod to the past but also completely customised to emphasise the new direction. The little people on the landscapes represent the lifestyle component.

What challenges did you face when creating the design?

The printing and reproduction of the colours and textures on pretty 'run of the mill' stocks had to be consistent, which was challenging, plus different items were printed at different factories in China, which meant getting consistent reproduction was very challenging, but the guys from O'Kelly Group did an amazing job.

If you could pick one aspect of the finished design that you like the most, what would it be and why?

I love the colours and textures. It's very different to Huxtaburger's original brand, however, in some way it feels somewhat like it's always been their brand, which is a really positive thing for them. They feel like they really own it.

FOOD

Bembos Fast food delivery
Infinito infinito.pe

ICHIRYU Udon house
Centre Creative Ltd centrecreative.com

Polu Poke Restaurant
Caterina Bianchini Design caterinabianchini.com

Elementary! Delivery Service Pizza, sushi, noodles & sandwiches
Dmitry Neal dmitryneal.ru

Summer of Pizza Pizza
Francesc Moret Studio francescmoret.com

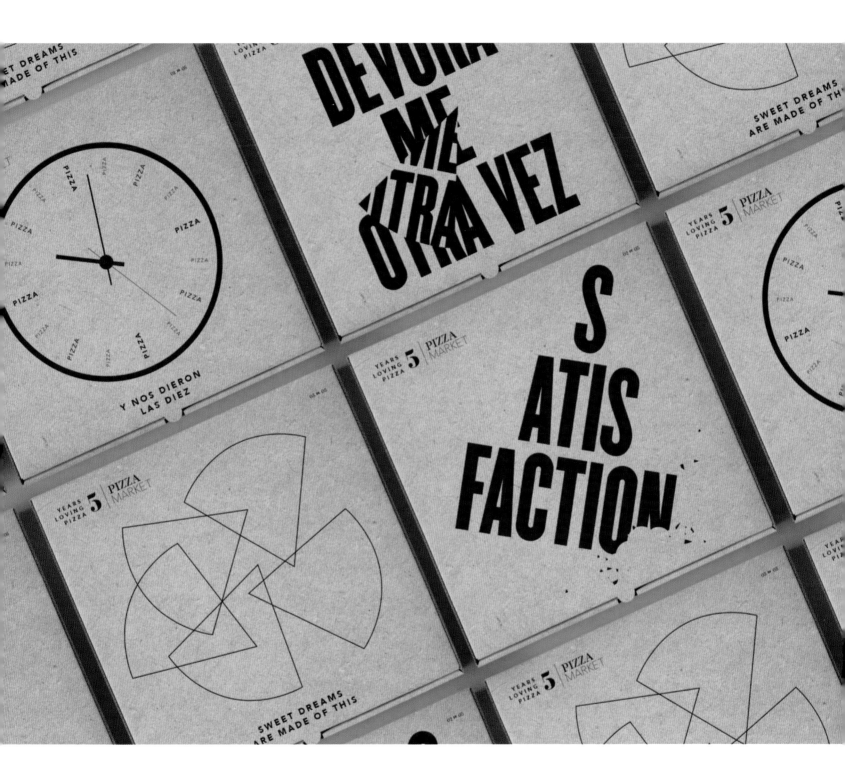

Five Years Loving Pizza Pizza
Francesc Moret Studio francescmoret.com

Rain or Shine Ice cream
Glasfurd & Walker
glasfurdandwalker.com

Mister Artisanal ice cream
Brief brief-studio.com

Selva Nevada Ice cream
Siegenthaler &Co siegenthaler.co **Photo** Lucho Mariño

FOOD

15

MiiRO Lollies
IWANT iwantdesign.co.uk

Bamsrudlåven Gårdsis Ice cream
OlssønBarbieri olssonbarbieri.com

Gorky Park
Ice Creams

~~~~~~~~~~~~~~~~~~~~~~~

Art Director Misha Gannushkin
Design Anastasia Genkina
behance.net/AnastasiaGenkina

**The designers wanted
to make something fresh
and yet with a friendly
and playful heart.**

This ice cream has been a treat that has
become inseparable from a walk in the
Moscow Gorky Park for decades. The
special taste of creamy vanilla and waffle
cone became a childhood memory for
several generations and the brand has
remained true to the old fashioned recipe.
The designers wanted to make something fresh
and yet with a friendly and playful heart,
that would contain the cultural heritage
associated with the park. Eye-catching
colours and patterns perform two tasks:
they correspond with a feeling of each
flavour and associate themselves with
leisure, open air and fun.
The wrap-arounds were printed on a thin,
old-fashioned butter-paper using
Pantone colours.

KUTE CAKE Cakes
IWANT iwantdesign.co.uk

Xoclad High-end pastry
& confectionery
Anagrama anagrama.com
Photo Caroga Foto /
carogafoto.com

Troufa Pastry & Bakery
Pastry & bakery
Luminous Design Group luminous.gr

Flour & Salt Bakery Food & beverage
Pentagram pentagram.com

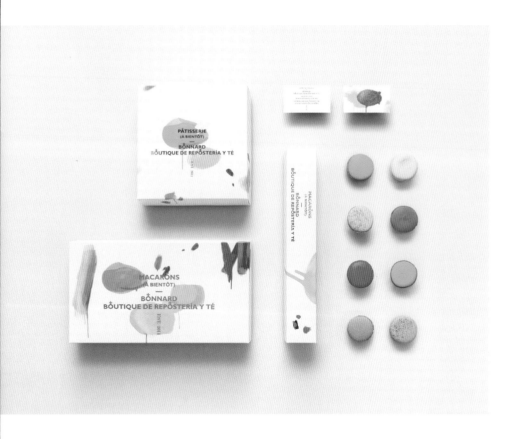

Bonnard

~~~~~~~~~~~~~~~~~~~~~~~~~~~~~~~~~~~

Anagrama
anagrama.com

The brand's distinct brush strokes and colour selection are based on Pierre Bonnard's post-impressionist paintings.

Bonnard is a Mexican, French-inspired tea and confectionery shop. The brand's distinct brush strokes and colour selection are based on Pierre Bonnard's post-impressionist paintings. The simple art direction, together with French words and phonetics, round up the brand's gallic concept effortlessly, spontaneously and efficiently.

Anagrama's approach with clean, sans-serif typography, gives Bonnard a luxurious feel, mostly associated with high-end fashion brands. The gold foil stamp and clean type directly contrasts, and at the same time elevates, the informal paint marks. The rounded cross icon detail, found in the wording, relates to the shapes of macaroons, one of Bonnard's prime delicacies.

Photo Caroga Foto / carogafoto.com

Maitre Choux Choux pastries
& desserts
MONOGRAM monogramlondon.com

FOOD

Vete-Katten Bakery & café
The Studio the-studio.se

Belle Epoque Patisserie Patisserie
Mind Design minddesign.co.uk

Leontiadis Family
Greek pita bread
Luminous Design Group
luminous.gr

FOOD

Amado

〰〰〰〰〰〰〰〰〰〰〰〰〰〰〰〰〰〰〰〰

Anagrama
anagrama.com

A visual solution that takes the fine art of traditional artisan bakery and contrasts it with a modernist aesthetic.

'Amado' by Hyatt is a Mexican artisan bakery and candy boutique specialised in typical, regional products characterised by their flavours, colours and textures. Hyatt reached out to Anagrama to develop a branding identity for the new boutique, opening in its hotel lobby.

Amado by Hyatt strives to bring together both the romantic and classic spirits of Amado Nervo's poetry and the modernist style of Mexican architect Luis Barragán.

Anagrama's branding proposal takes the two iconic Mexican minds and their fellow characteristics and creates a visual solution that takes the fine art of traditional artisan bakery and contrasts it with a modernist aesthetic, that guarantees the brand stands out among others. The design company's intention was to, 'avoid falling into typical Mexican clichés'.

Photo Caroga Foto / carogafoto.com

FOOD

Sorger Bakery
Bruch—Idee&Form studiobruch.com

Lune Croissanterie Croissants & pastries
A Friend of Mine afom.com.au

Coffee & Co. Cafeteria on a cruise ship
Bond Creative Agency bond-agency.com

WELL Coffee Vegetarian café concept
Bond Creative Agency bond-agency.com

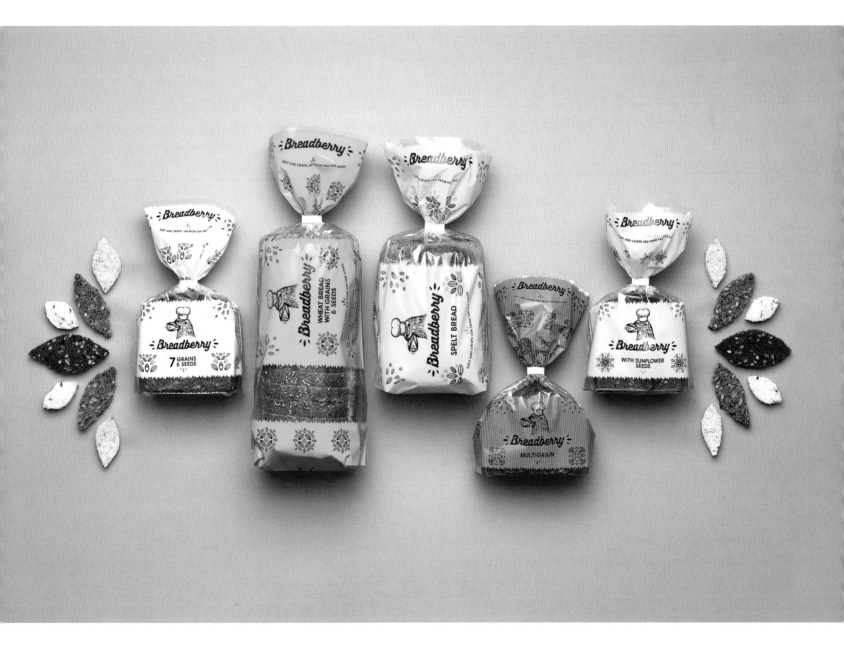

BulkBarn Canada's largest bulk foods retailer
Leo Burnett Design, Toronto leoburnettdesign.ca

お米にぬくもりが使ってる
しろくまのお米

Shirokuma No Okome Rice
Frame inc. frame-d.jp

Gimme a Hug Rice
RONG rong-design.com

nourish

Chewy
Blueberry
Apple
Granola Bites

100 Cal.
Per Serving

NET WT.
4 OZ. (113G)

Nourish Snacks

~~~~~~~~~~~~~~~~~~~~~~~~~~~~~~~~

COLLINS
wearecollins.com

Nourish Snacks enjoyed strong initial success with their granola treats, but they were eager – and ready – to become a stronger national challenger in the snack category. COLLINS was invited to help Nourish Snacks do just that by reimagining and relaunching the company.

To design a more magnetic brand for Nourish Snacks, they first set out to better understand what now drives people's behavior in snacking. Through ethnographic research, in-home visits and shop-along trips with customers – as well as category research and interviews with key company stakeholders and retailers – COLLINS identified an idea that allowed them to unlock a new, defining value for Nourish Snacks.

The new brand identity and packaging draws from that idea – and aims to intertwine the surprising with the familiar. COLLINS were inspired by memories from when, 'snacking was less complicated, less worrisome and, well, more fun'.

The bold diagonals on the front of the new packaging come from the stripes found on snacks sold at the circus, carnivals and baseball games. Striped popcorn and peanut boxes, cotton candy and ice cream cones, 'all of them held the promise of delight'. COLLINS borrowed from this familiar, whimsical language to invite people to try something surprising, new, different… and a lot better for you.

The Primal Kitchen Paleo bars
Midday Studio Ltd middaystudio.com

SMCo. Gourmet muesli & granola
Peter Jay Deering peterjaydeering.com

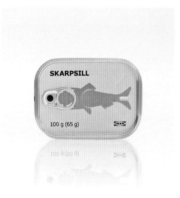

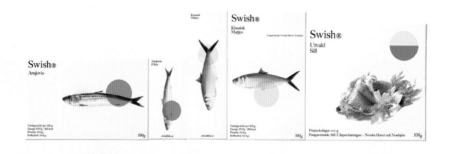

Springs' Smokery Smoked salmon
Distil Studio distilstudio.co.uk

IKEA Food
Stockholm Design Lab stockholmdesignlab.se

Swish Seafood
empatia helloempatia.com

Zamora Biltong Meat snacks
makebardo makebardo.com

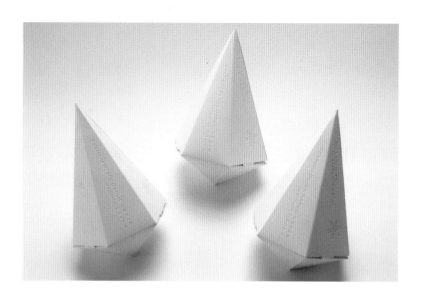

Towada Premium Black Garlic
Garlic
Keiko Akatsuka & Associates
keikored.tv

Fuwafuwa Mozzarella Cheese
Mozzarella cheese
Terashima Design Co. tera-d.net

Corphes Organic herbs
Luminous Design Group luminous.gr

Feinschmeck Soup
Isabella Thaller isabellathaller.com **Photo** Christian Pitschl

Feinschmeck

SELLERIE-BIRNENSUPPE
MIT SAFRAN

MM by Mimo Gourmet Spanish products
Campbell Hay campbellhay.com

Peakfarm Food
Grand Deluxe grand-deluxe.com

Hurly Burly Fermented raw slaws
Midday Studio Ltd middaystudio.com

Pomodoro Pop Tomatoes
nju:comunicazione njucomunicazione.com

Saints, Pummarulelle & Paccheri Tomatoes
nju:comunicazione njucomunicazione.com

Cortijo Abades Extra virgin olive oil
Buenaventura Studio buenaventura.pro

1 L

250 ml

500 ml

Tenute Librandi Olive oil
nju:comunicazione njucomunicazione.com

Orazio's Olive oil
Brief brief-studio.com

Alivu Extra virgin olive oil
Solid Studio solidstudio.it

Auro Olive Oil Olive oil
nju:comunicazione
njucomunicazione.com

Olleum Terra Graeca Olive oil
talc design studio talcdesignstudio.com

Danish Selection

Kontrapunkt
kontrapunkt.com

Inspired by classic alcohol labels, Kontrapunkt designed a bold, typographic design that balanced modernity and tradition.

Kontrapunkt were aware that a new product in a traditional category needs a distinct design. In shelves packed with white labels, fruit images and ornament, the design company gave these alcoholic, fruit spreads a round label with a bold and characteristic colour palette, that made the high fruit and berry percentage the focal point.

Inspired by classic alcohol labels, Kontrapunkt designed a bold, typographic design that balanced modernity and tradition, to make the small, but powerful, jams stand out on the shelves.

Rufino 1949 Jams & preserves
Buenaventura Studio buenaventura.pro

Summerhill Market Poached pears
Blok Design blokdesign.com

JammyYummy Jams
Hey heystudio.es **Photo** Roc Canals

Drink

"We agreed early on that these were canvases to be played with, to be stylish, dynamic and fun."

IWANT

Niche

~~~~~~

IWANT
iwantdesign.co.uk

Talk us through the design process that you went through for this project.
There was a lot discussion with the client throughout the project about its positioning, who was it talking to, what stores do we want to see it in etc. We spent a lot of time walking around different stores looking at tea and other products and brands we felt Niche should be aligned with. We also looked at boutique and concept stores that didn't, or wouldn't usually, stock tea, and started to think about it as a lifestyle product, something any kind of stylish high-end store would consider stocking. So when thinking about the design, we wanted something with immediate visual impact that would make browsers stop and look, we wanted it to be exciting and unique in its sphere.

What was one of the biggest goals you set out to achieve with the Niche packaging and how did you accomplish it?

We wanted people to take notice immediately – this intentionally isn't a supermarket product, so to achieve volume sales we needed the net to be cast wide, we needed the product to be visible to as many consumers and stockists as possible, as quickly as possible, to give the product some traction. The design, the packaging, the photography were all geared to have a big visual impact, to be blogable and share worthy, to create brand awareness. So far, this is working above expectation.

How did you develop the graphic style?

We agreed early on that these were canvases to be played with, to be stylish, dynamic and fun. The flavour profiles were still in development when we began experimenting and we agreed the designs didn't need to be literal representations of the ingredients. Thereafter, it was a process of experimenting with ideas and techniques until we settled on a range of ideas.

What elements of the design do you feel speak of the products premium quality?

The uncoated paper that covers the tubes is soft and tactile, the subtle gold foiled logo, the treatment of copy all shout premium. But sometimes it's the little details like the printed tags on the bags and the printed inner spool on the tubes, that show an attention to detail that you may not get on a lesser product.

How did you keep the bright colours, text and background patterns from overwhelming the consumer?

Sometimes overwhelming the consumer might be the answer. If there are shelves of underwhelming packages to choose from, you want to be the opposite, you want to jump out and say, 'look at me!' Some supermarkets absolutely don't want that, they want uniformity, but how do you infer personality or a point of difference, if you look the same as everything else. There are certain legal requirements for food and beverage packaging that can't be avoided, beyond that, we wanted to show as little information as possible. There is a small description of the blend and a short quote on each.

Melez Tea Tea gift boxes
Atelier Nese Nogay ateliernesenogay.com

**KaiMon – Taiwan Tea House Spring
Gift Box** Tea
Erica Su behance.net/13smile

GREEN TEA powder

net wt 30g

1/6

UKIYO

CEREMONIAL GRADE MATCHA

UKIYO Matcha
IWANT iwantdesign.co.uk

Teabox Beverage
Pentagram pentagram.com

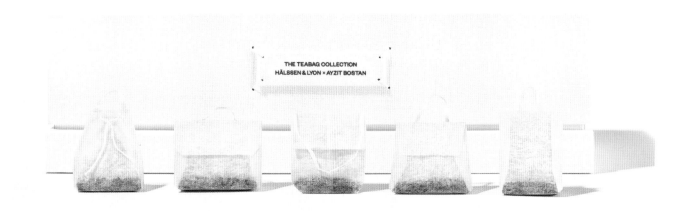

Hälssen & Lyon – The Teabag Collection Teabags
KOREFE. Kolle Rebbe Form und Entwicklung korefe.de

Twig Teas Tea
Studio Thomas studiothomas.co.uk

ChariTea Iced tea drink
The Studio the-studio.se

DRINK

Stempels' Slowbrew Cold brew coffee
Bureau Haider bureauhaider.com

Sandows Cold brew coffee
Studio Thomas studiothomas.co.uk

Hatch Cold Brew Coffee
Cold brew coffee
Tung madebytung.com

Archer Farms

〰〰〰〰〰〰〰〰〰〰〰〰〰

COLLINS
wearecollins.com

The unified grid system at the top of each bag indicates key attributes across name, flavour cues and origin.

Target was the first mass-retailer to offer fair trade coffee to its millions of guests. Knowing their guests are increasingly curious about product sourcing and large-scale impact, the brand recently revitalised their assortment of Archer Farms coffee to better reflect the product story 'from farm to cup' and partnered with COLLINS to do so.

Coffee is a complicated category for guests to navigate; not only are there a number of cues that must be taken into account across flavour, roast and origin, but beans and single-serve cups also sit tightly packed, side-by-side on shelf.

The unified grid system at the top of each bag indicates key attributes across name, flavour cues and origin. COLLINS invited a number of illustrators to create a scalable, custom solution to showcase the varieties of coffee, emphasising how and where the beans are grown.

Finefood Deli & café
The Studio the-studio.se

Father Coffee Single origin, speciality coffee beans
Nicholas Christowitz
nicholaschristowitz.com

Deluca Coffee Café & roastery
Christopher Doyle & Co. christopherdoyle.co

Vispera Coffee Coffee
Stockholm Design Lab stockholmdesignlab.se

Square One Coffee Roasters Coffee beans & ground coffee
Pop & Pac pop-pac.com

DRINK

BIG BOSS PALM Coconut water soda
Ayesha Sherriffs ayeshasherriffs.com

DRINK

Nakai Farm Apple juice
Terashima Design Co. tera-d.net

Suikahime Soft drink
ShakeDesign shake-design.com

Henri Sodas Soft drink
Caserne studiocaserne.ca

DALSTON'S Non-alcoholic beverages
B&B studio ltd bandb-studio.co.uk

Ashridge Drinks Alcoholic beverages & soft drinks
Buddy buddycreative.com

Alda Iceland Natural, healthy lemonade with marine collagen
Iceland Ocean Cluster sjavarklasinn.is **Milja Korpela** miljaemilia.com

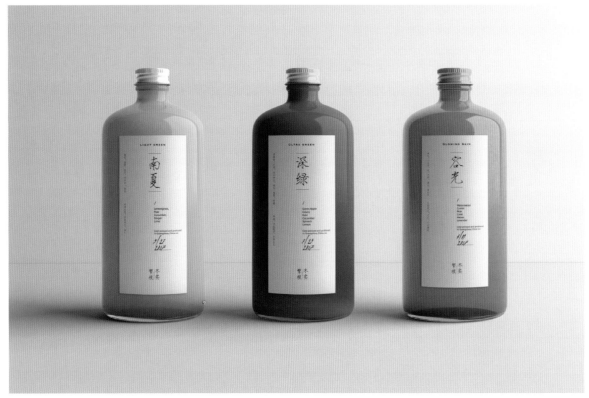

Fruitvale Juice
Studio Once studioonce.com

Seafarers Cocktails & sodas
Inhouse inhouse.nz

Hopt Non-alcoholic beverage
Inhouse inhouse.nz

Jinnam Agricultural Corporation
Jinnam omija juice
CFC contentformcontext.com

JUS · Juice Up Saigon Cold-pressed juice
M — N Associates m-n.associates

Raw Co. Cold-pressed juice
Pupila pupila.co **Photo** Camila Jurado

Lemonaid Soft drink
The Studio the-studio.se

Oroblanco Kefir & kumis yogurt drink
Pupila pupila.co
Photo Mario Gómez, Black Pepper

J+ Cold-pressed drinks
empatia helloempatia.com

Alpokaqua

〜〜〜〜〜〜〜〜〜〜〜〜〜〜〜〜〜〜〜〜

Kissmiklos
kissmiklos.com

The designer's intention was to design a label with an optical play. If we look through the bottle, we see the mountains blurred on the other side of the label.

Over 15 thousand years ago the underground mineral water reservoir of Alpokaqua was created in the one mile-high Alps, where it remained protected from environmental pollution.

Kissmiklos changed the 'A' within the logo to a stylised mountain icon and the Alps visually reoccur in the label's illustrations, too. The designer's intention was to design a label with an optical play. If we look through the bottle, we see the mountains blurred on the other side of the label.

Photo Eszter Sarah

Akka Water
Stockholm Design Lab stockholmdesignlab.se **Photo** Marcus Hansen

Miin Rice wine Rice wine
CFC contentformcontext.com

PYT Pét-Nat Rosé Wine
Fredericus l'Ami theycallmefred.com

Pulchella Winery/
Paso Robles Wines Wine
Hype Type Studio hypetype.studio

Bodega
Los Cedros

~~~~~~~~~~~~~~~~~~~~~~~~~~~~~~~~~~~~

Anagrama
anagrama.com

The packaging composition recalls the landscapes around 'El Cedrito' winery.

Bodega Los Cedros, represents a Mexican vineyard, located in the mountains of Arteaga, Coahuila. It was originally motivated by the passion and dream of a family to produce high quality wines within a 100 year old setting, 'El Cedrito'.

Based on the geographical location of the mountains where the vineyard is located, Anagrama's brand solution highlights characteristic components of the area such as climate, altitude, flora and fauna.

The sans serif typography adds modernity, while the script gesture preserves a more organic touch, suggesting the way the brand contrasts simplicity and elegance.

Anagrama included a neutral colour selection to highlight the diverse wine colour tones and accentuate the contrast between bottle and label. The packaging composition recalls the landscapes around 'El Cedrito' winery.

Photo Caroga Foto / carogafoto.com

El Hans Wine
Buenaventura Studio buenaventura.pro

Waddesdon Wine – Château Lafite & Château Mouton Gift Set Wine
Paul Belford Ltd paulbelford.com

Kinoene Apple Japanese junmai ginjo sake
tegusu Inc. tegusu.com

Kincsem Kastély Winery Wine
Kissmiklos kissmiklos.com

79

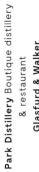

Park Distillery Boutique distillery
& restaurant
Glasfurd & Walker
glasfurdandwalker.com

Hellstrøm Aquavit Alcoholic
beverage/spirits
OlssønBarbieri olssonbarbieri.com

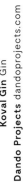

Koval Gin Gin
Dando Projects dandoprojects.com

Verdant Dry Gin Gin
Graphical House graphicalhouse.com

Tequila Casa Pujol 87 Tequila
Anagrama anagrama.com **Photo** Caroga Foto / carogafoto.com

Blossa Hantverksglögg Mulled wine
The Studio the-studio.se

Wild Island Gin Gin
Thirst thirstcraft.com

Bonnie & Clyde Gin

The Adventures of Pearly Yon
pearlyyon.com

All the type on these labels has been created from scratch. The design was very much inspired by the 1930's era.

These labels were designed by Pearly Yon for a micro distillery in Belgium. The brief required a pair of labels that would be applied to a limited run of hand-crafted gin. The sweeter tasting gin was called Bonnie and the stronger tasting gin was Clyde. Together the notorious two needed to, 'dominate shelf presence behind the bar and come across as classy, refined and of the highest quality'.

All the type on these labels has been created from scratch. The design was very much inspired by the 1930's era. Each bottle has been screen printed directly onto the glass, using four colours and a foil. The gin has been hand-crafted in small quantities. Each bottle is numbered by hand and only 500 bottles of each have ever been produced.

Lillevik Alpine Cider
makebardo makebardo.com

Golden Axe Apple Cider Cider
Mikey Burton mikeyburton.com

Miłosław Warzy Śmiało Beer
Ostecx Créative ostecx.com

Szyszak Beer
Ostecx Créative ostecx.com

Kaiju Beer Beer
Mikey Burton mikeyburton.com

Clapton Micro Brewery Beer
Yang Ripol Design Studio
yangripol.com

86

Citizen Beer Beer
Monday Design mondaydesign.co.za

Strawman Brewery Beer
Patrick Fry patrickfry.co.uk

Bullfinch Brewery Beer
George Simkin georgesimkin.com

Brok Beer
Ostecx Créative ostecx.com

Cargo Lager Beer
makebardo makebardo.com

Rrëy Beer
Firmalt firmalt.com

Brussels Beer Project Crowdfunded beer
COAST coast-agency.com

O/O Brewing Long Boil Barley Wine Beer
Lundgren+Lindqvist lundgrenlindqvist.se

C10 Beer
Kissmiklos kissmiklos.com

DRINK

DRINK

Sample Brew Beer
Longton longtondesign.com

Grain Brewery Beer
Creative Giant creativegiant.co.uk

Six Mile Bridge Beer
Monday Design mondaydesign.co.za

Zwakala Beer
Monday Design mondaydesign.co.za

Tokyo Dry Alcoholic beverage
Inhouse inhouse.nz

Vocation Brewery Craft Lager Alcoholic drink/craft lager
Robot Food robot-food.com

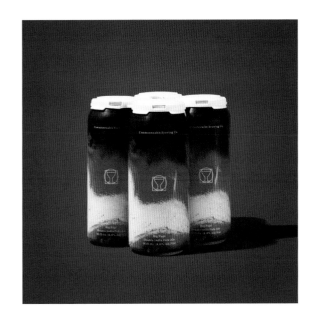

Big Papi Craft beer
Thirst thirstcraft.com

Noon Whistle Brewing Company
Craft beer
Zimmer-Design Inc.
zimmer-design.com

DRINK

Great Dane Craft beer
Zimmer-Design Inc. zimmer-design.com

Emergency Drinking Beer Beer
Office of Brothers bros.family

Kinkura Craft beer
nendo nendo.jp
Photo Akihiro Yoshida

Patagonia Long Root Ale Beer
Hype Type Studio hypetype.studio

DRINK

Cosmetics

"Sometimes package design is about the presentation of an unexpected form. Sometimes it's just about presenting an expected form in an unexpected way. They are equally rewarding."

Athletics

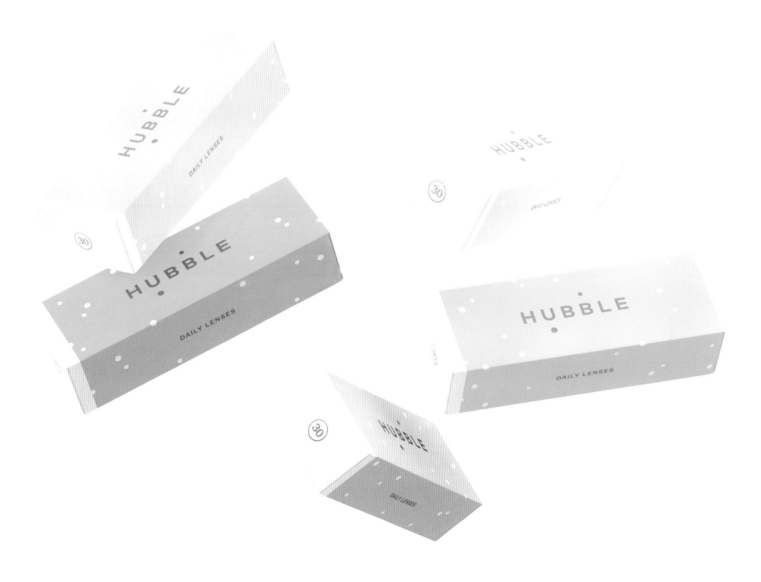

Hubble

Athletics
athleticsnyc.com

COSMETICS

What was the brief for this project and how did the opportunity come about?

When the team at Hubble approached us, they knew they could share prescription contacts with the world at half the price of what was currently available. What they needed from us was a construct that supported and introduced their new brand to both a healthcare system and a public that was justifiably concerned about trying new things when it came to vision health. Weeks of discussion gave way to the development of a strategic platform and a name that ultimately informed where we went with the design.

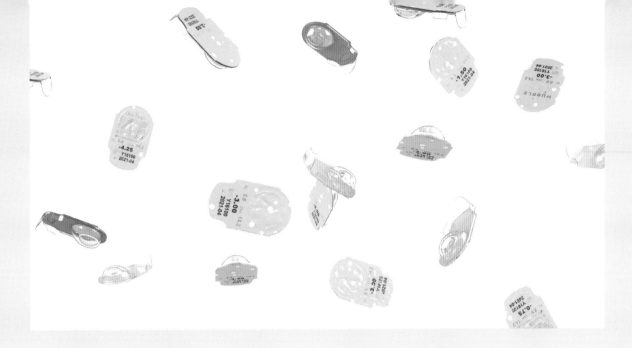

Walk us through the design process that you went through for this project.

From the start, a name like 'Hubble' offered many possibilities – clarity, science, precision, etc. – but the instinct was to take it to a softer place. There is enough technical imagery within this category. What about dots? Are they bubbles, or star clusters, or lenses… maybe they are just dots? Maybe they are more. And colour – everyone else is cool blues. We wanted to be a little cool but mostly uncool, which can be cool too.

What challenges did you face when creating the design?

As a direct-to-consumer product, cost efficiencies drove a lot of the early decision making. We knew we'd need to make the most of off-the-shelf solutions, so we worked with a great partner to make sure we had the nicest options available.

How did you balance stripping the packaging down and making attractive products consumers would want in their home?

We wanted the packaging to trigger the same words they may use to describe their ideal lenses: soft, clean, light. If they glance at the packaging and their brains make these connections, this is enough.

What information did you feel was necessary to include and to leave off?

Beyond the initial unboxing, the needs of the wearer are relatively simple: 'does this go in my left eye or my right eye?' That is a small amount of work for design. However, this is also a health product, so doctors and lawyers can happily find any need-to-know information on the lower side or interior of the box.

How is a client's brand identity enhanced by effective design?

Packaging should only ever be an extension of the broader brand rationale. Some brands want to communicate that they very much deserve a leading place among their competitors, while others may feel it's better to operate on the fringes as a new, alternative consideration. For Hubble, it was the latter, but effectiveness can be found in either approach.

Share one lesson that you learned while developing the packaging.

Sometimes package design is about the presentation of an unexpected form. Sometimes it's just about presenting an expected form in an unexpected way. They are equally rewarding.

Daughter of the Land Body oil
Dando Projects dandoprojects.com

Ena Natural skincare range
Ortolan ortolan.com.au

naturaglacé Cosmetics
nendo nendo.jp **Photo** Kei Iwasaki

Freshly Baked Tanning foam
Design Happy designhappy.co.uk

Daub & Bauble Bath & body products
Wink wink-mpls.com

Parko Organic skincare line
Caterina Bianchini Design caterinabianchini.com

Minerals Natural Care
Health & beauty
Super Magic Friend
supermagicfriend.com

C'est Ça Handmade soap
Aleksandar Cvetković, Inc.
aleksandarcvetkovic.com

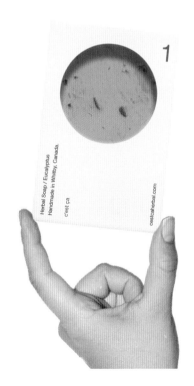

Sphynx

~~~~~~~~~~~~~~~~~~~~~~~~~~~~~~~~~~~

Anagrama
anagram.com

The packaging stands out due to its shape and intense colour palette, referencing the energy and joviality of the brand.

Sphynx is a product that seeks to shift the perception of traditional and complicated beauty routines. It comprises a shaving device, with a simple mechanism that can be set in one of four positions for its use. The first, unveils a rechargeable water spray that helps refresh the skin before shaving. The second, includes a moisturising soap to moisturise the skin. The third, shows the razors employed for shaving. The fourth stores a piece of soap.

The packaging stands out due to its shape and intense colour palette, referencing the energy and joviality of the brand. The brand pattern is inspired by circular polka dots that create a relaxed but dynamic texture, complementing the brand's graphic communication. Gotham typography was selected for its geometric, readable and timeless style, complementing the modern tone of voice required by the brand.

Photo Caroga Foto / carogafoto.com

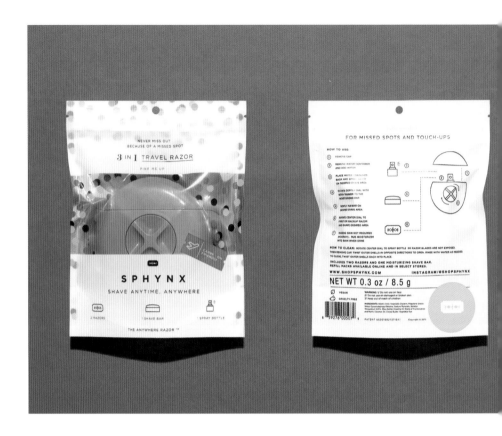

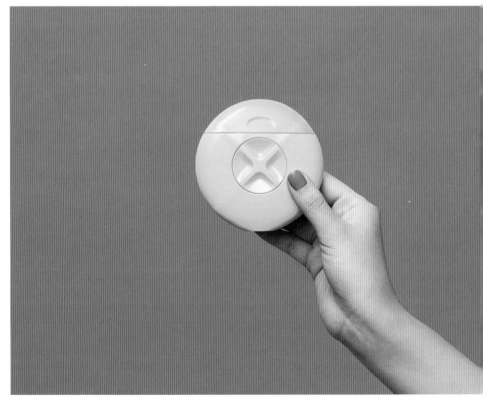

Eyes Cream Concealer
**KOREFE. Kolle Rebbe Form und
Entwicklung** korefe.de

dan Soap & facial mask
HOUTH houth.tw

Cosmic Canter Beauty skincare
Studio Calypso
studiocalypso.com.au

COSRX Make Me Lovely Cushion
Cosmetics
TRIANGLE-STUDIO
triangle-studio.co.kr

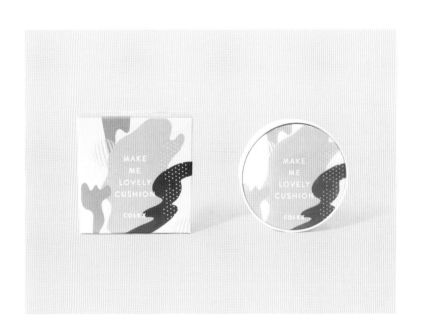

COSMETICS

Il Makiage Makeup Cosmetics
Studio Koniak koniakdesign.com

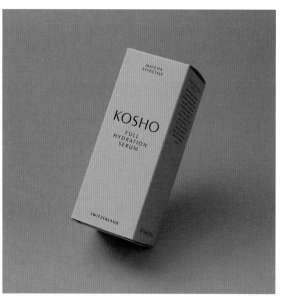

Kosho Cosmetics Cosmetics
Bureau Collective bureaucollective.ch

Hanskin Cosmetics
CFC contentformcontext.com

Stellar

Bruce Mau Design
brucemaudesign.com

Taking visual inspiration from the cosmos, the brand identity and name allude to starry constellations.

Stellar is a high-performance makeup brand that delivers across all skin colours, with a particular focus on medium tones. The line features a full range of products that includes foundations, concealers, loose powders, blushes, lipsticks and mascaras.

Bruce Mau Design took visual inspiration from the cosmos. The brand identity and name allude to starry constellations. The word mark includes a dot that, 'echoes both the North Star and a beauty mark' and the colours used, 'reflect the inclusive nature of the brand'. Meanwhile, the use of black and white represents, 'night and day, while a secondary opalescent palette used on the packaging vibrates across the full spectrum of light'.

Working with the client, the designers developed all brand touchpoints – positioning and story, name, visual identity, website, packaging, campaign photography and collateral.

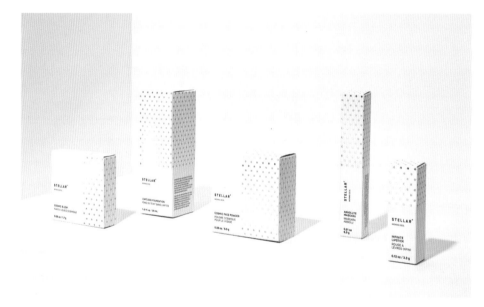

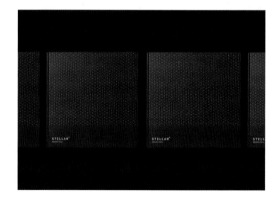

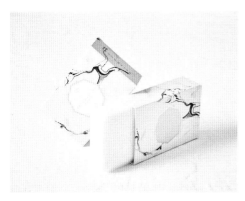

Tulura Skincare
Build studio.build

Waterworks Apothecary
DCO Partners sdcopartners.com

MySkin Face cream
KOREFE. Kolle Rebbe Form und Entwicklung korefe.de

COSMETICS

Marc Jacobs Beauty – Kiss Pop Collection Cosmetics
Established establishednyc.com

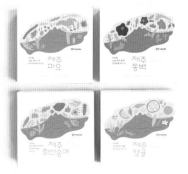

CIRACLE From jeju Cosmetics
TRIANGLE-STUDIO
triangle-studio.co.kr

Jack Wills, Hope Cove Fragrance
Sarah Thorne sarahthorne.co.uk

Hanami Cosmetics
Eve Warren evewarren.com

REN – Christmas Gift Sets Skincare
Kangan Arora kanganarora.com

COSMETICS

C.LAVIE Cosmetics
Agence LaPetiteGrosse lapetitegrosse.com **Photo** Paul Rousteau

COSRX Mini Packaging for Samples Cosmetics
TRIANGLE-STUDIO triangle-studio.co.kr

Karen Walker – Runaway Fragrance
Inhouse inhouse.nz

Kiehl's Cosmetics
Craig & Karl craigandkarl.com

Minois Paris Natural care line for babies & kids
Borho Studio borho.studio

27 87 Perfumes Perfumery
Ingrid Picanyol Studio ingridpicanyol.com

Palermo Skincare
SDCO Partners sdcopartners.com

PLAYA Haircare
Manual manualcreative.com

COSMETICS

Sai-Sei for Space.NK
Home spa essentials
BOB Design bobdesign.co.uk

Zarko Perfume – Cloud Collection
Perfume
Homework homework.dk
Photo Günther Egger /
guentheregger.at

Belmacz Beauty Cosmetics
Mind Design minddesign.co.uk **Photo** Franck Allais

Onomie Beauty Beauty products
Homework homework.dk

Custommade – Fragrance Create your own scent – collection
of four custom blend fragrances
Homework homework.dk

Homework – Le Parfum Homework Le Parfum Collector Limited Edition
Homework homework.dk

Aria Cosmetics Make-up
Hawaii Hawaiidesign.co.uk

H by LPN (La Peau Nu) Fragrance
KLEIN carstenklein.com

COSMETICS

The Soap Co. – Hand Wash & Hand
Lotion Toiletries
Paul Belford Ltd paulbelford.com

REF Haircare
Kurppa Hosk kurppahosk.com

Verso Skincare Skincare
The Studio the-studio.se

Topshop Make Up Cosmetics
Sarah Thorne sarahthorne.co.uk

REN – Mail Order Packaging Skincare
Kangan Arora kanganarora.com

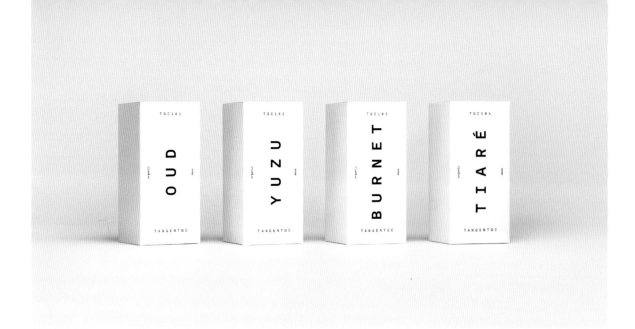

TANGENT GC Organic Soaps Hand soap
Carl Nas Associates carlnas.com

SG Plus Repellent Aroma Mist
Repellent mist for mosquitos
Jiyoun Kim Studio jiyounkim.com

DESIGNTORGET Home Care Soap, detergent
& hand soap
Carl Nas Associates carlnas.com

Confectionery

"We can only design to the brand's true traits and values. It is so important to discover and define these first. After these are defined, the design is almost a straight-forward explanation."

Rice Creative

Maison Marou Saigon
Rice Creative

Maison Marou Saigon

Rice Creative
rice-creative.com

What was the brief for this project and how did the opportunity come about?

We have been helping Marou Chocolate develop their brand from very early on, here in Vietnam. After the packaged products had begun finding shelves around the world, it became an issue that most of the product was being exported to Europe, the US and Japan. Marou wished to make a stronger connection with their local audience and have a place where they could invite people to the brand and show, by living example, their amazing story.

It was also time for Marou to experiment more and consider new products. We realised that the opening of the first store would not only provide an incredible opportunity for the brand to offer a complete story, but it could be something immersive and interactive. Maison Marou became a full-on inner city chocolate factory, where the chocolatiers could experiment with new flavours and textures. New chocolate bars could be offered to Marou's clientele and the ones that performed well at the location, would be put into full production for export.

Walk us through the design process that you went through for this project.

The process was about going back to the beginning. When we started with Marou, we knew the biggest opportunity we had to explain the unique story to the world would be the chocolate bar itself. The brand owners had always wanted to have a downtown public factory, but early on, it simply was not on the cards. A lot of the brand identity early on, was developed to work as a packaging range. That packaging range had to convey a lot of the story. Creating a space for them, allowed us to unfold so much – we were able to craft spaces and experiences around unique parts of the Marou story.

What were the technical issues in creating the packaging?

The packaging was technically straight-forward. Once the design had taken shape, conveying the concept, it was a matter of printing a simple sheet of paper. Of course the sheets are beautifully screen printed to align with the hand-made nature of the product, but screen printing is not technically challenging in Vietnam, where it is a widely practiced printing method. We did, however, have to help convince a local printer to move from printing mostly wedding invitations, to printing thousands of chocolate wrappers.

What elements of the design do you feel speak to the product's high quality?

Everything Marou had done in the beginning was new and invented from the ground up and the design work is the same. We take a similar 'journey', essentially doing everything the hard way. We looked at no existing reference points, other than local and historical inspiration we dug up in our research. From there, everything was invented and made by hand. Every aspect is custom designed, but made with great care and precision. This is true of everything from the packaging, to the furniture and space itself.

What was the most challenging part of this project?

With so much to 'get out', restraint became an important practice. Maison Marou is a boutique, factory and café all-in-one. It also attempts to be a didactic place with a lot of takeaways. We had to keep stripping away, so that key aspects could communicate on their own and in unison. There was a real risk of information and design overload.

How is a client's brand identity enhanced by effective design?

We can only design to the brand's true traits and values. It is so important to discover and define these first. After these are defined, the design is almost a straightforward explanation. An effective design will introduce to the right audience, 'what the brand is all about', well.

What one aspect of the design do you feel especially proud of and why?

The space operates well, it works, but the over-all expression is that of an experimental place. Customers are invited 'along on the adventure'. The menu board in the spaces is made of interchangeable pieces that allow the chocolatiers to change it on a whim. The menu is the centerpiece of the front space and on top of being dynamic, is often carrying extra messaging. The place feels alive and ever-changing. This aspect of the design is one we are very proud of, we have not created a museum, but a living, breathing entity.

Mandarin Natural Chocolate Chocolate
Yuta Takahashi yutatakahashi.jp

Mast Night Chocolates Chocolate
Atlas designbyatlas.com **Creative Director** Astrid Stavro

Land Chocolate
Studio Thomas studiothomas.co.uk

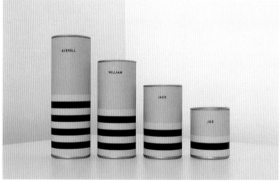

The Dalton Brothers
by Josep Maria Ribé Chocolate
Ingrid Picanyol Studio
ingridpicanyol.com

Milk Chocolate Coins Chocolate
Distil Studio distilstudio.co.uk

Cocoa Colony

~~~~~~~~~~~~~~~~~~~~~~~~~

Bravo
bravo.rocks

**On the packaging, gold
was embellished with great
intent to emphasise
the affection we have
for the product.**

Cocoa Colony is a chocolate brand that
tells the story of two brothers who
discovered the many benefits of cocoa
beans when they found themselves
stranded in Ecuador after their ship
capsized during the Colonial Period.
With its healing properties and delicious
aroma, the precious cocoa beans
became known as the 'Amazonian Gold'
when the brothers brought them back
to their homeland.

Bravo felt the need to retell the story in
elaborate details through meticulous
typography and material choices during
the creation of the brand. On the
packaging, gold was embellished with
great intent to emphasise the affection
we have for the product.

Bolonaf Chocolate
empatia helloempatia.com

Bibelot Boutique desserts, artisanal pastries & chocolates
A Friend of Mine afom.com.au

Brown Sugar 1st.'s Coco cookies Confectionery
Keiko Akatsuka & Associates keikored.tv

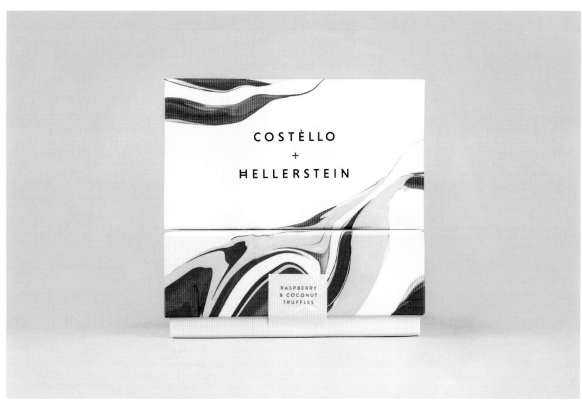

Costello & Hellerstein Confectionary
Robot Food robot-food.com

NEAT CONFECTIONS

GALLETAS DE MANTEQUILLA

TRIBUTO A:

ROSAS Y TÉ BLANCO

Delicados, fragantes, ligeros y florales, los tonos de las rosas y el té blanco se complementan y exaltan en la compañía del sabor lácteo de la mantequilla francesa.

CONT. NET. 130 GR.

NEAT CONFECTIONS

GALLETAS DE MANTEQUILLA

TRIBUTO A:

LIMÓN AMARILLO Y VAINILLA

El perfume suave y dulce de la vainilla mexicana profundiza la frescura cítrica, vibrante y floral del limón amarillo.

CONT. NET. 130 GR.

NEAT CONFECTIONS

GALLETAS DE MANTEQUILLA

TRIBUTO A:

EL ROMERO

Amaderado, cítrico, fragante, terroso y casi floral, el Romero mexicano es espectacular siempre.

CONT. NET. 130 GR.

NEAT CONFECTIONS

GALLETAS DE MANTEQUILLA

TRIBUTO A:

LAVANDA Y VAINILLA

Con notas florales y casi cítricas, el fuerte sabor de la lavanda encuentra su balance en la aromática vainilla mexicana que aporta su carácter único de madera y especias.

CONT. NET. 130 GR.

NEAT CONFECTIONS

Una ofrenda al gusto, elaborada con ingredientes que cortejan el placer por la comida.

ESTD · 2014

NEAT CONFECTIONS

Una ofrenda al gusto, elaborada con ingredientes que cortejan el placer por la comida.

ESTD · 2014

NEATCONFECTIONS.COM

NEAT CONFECTIONS

GALLETAS DE MANTEQUILLA

TRIBUTO A:

ROSAS Y TÉ BLANCO

Delicados, fragantes, ligeros y florales, los tonos de las rosas y el té blanco se complementan y exaltan en la compañía del sabor lácteo de la mantequilla francesa.

CONT. NET. 130 GR.

NEATCONFECTIONS.COM

Neat Confections Pastry shop
Anagrama anagrama.com
Photo Caroga Foto /
carogafoto.com

CONFECTIONERY

Fruna Candy
Brandlab brandlab.pe

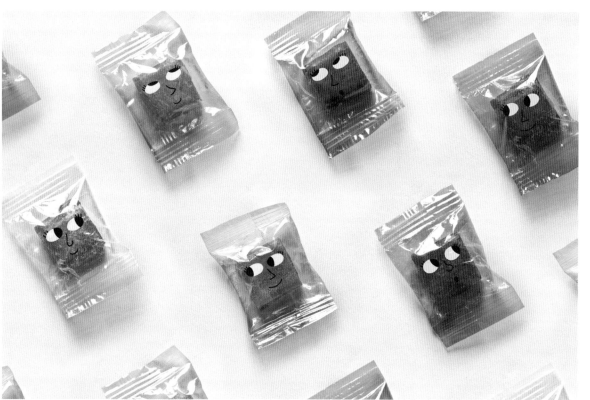

Le Caramelle Candy
Happycentro happycentro.it

The Marshmallowist Handcrafted Marshmallows Confectionary
Veronica Lethorn/No one

HEY YUM! Organic candy
Studio Arhoj arhoj.com

100% Natural Raw chocolate brownies
Midday Studio Ltd middaystudio.com

Wakabiyori for Cozy Corner Co.,Ltd. Confectionery
AWATSUJIdesign awatsujidesign.com

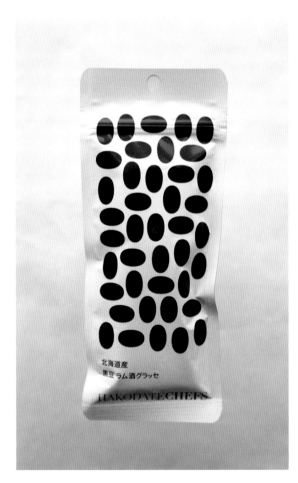

Hokadate Chefs, Black Beans Glacé
Confectionery
Terashima Design Co. tera-d.net

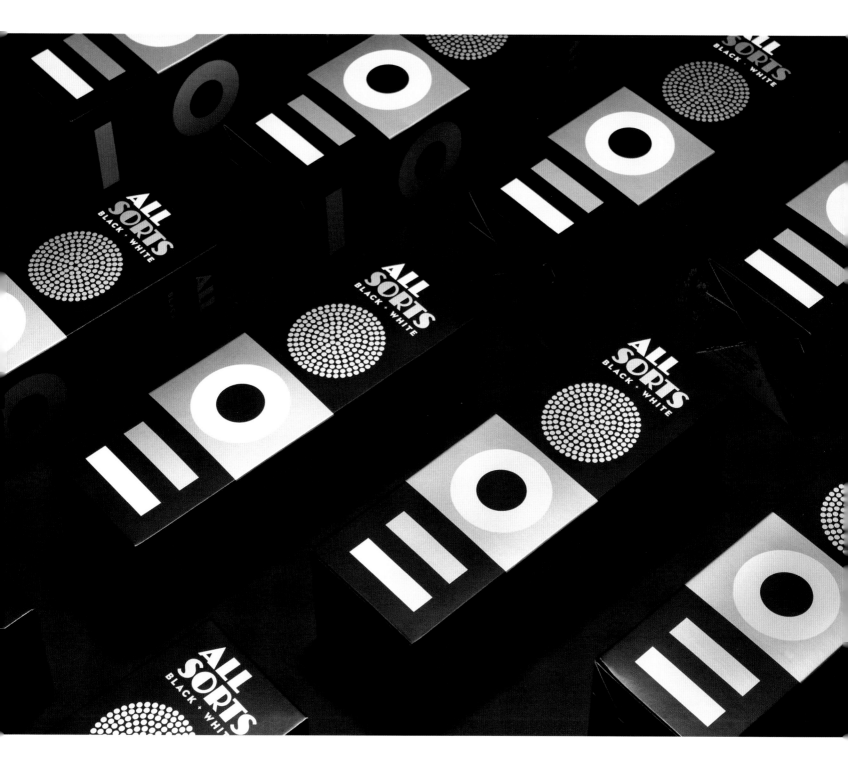

Fashion

"Effective identity design is the greatest tool to communicate a brand's personality. When done right, it sets the brand apart from the competition, creates memorable connections and adds value to the brand as a whole."

Perky Bros.

Perky Bros.
perkybros.com

January Moon

~~~~~~

Perky Bros.
perkybros.com

Can you tell me a little about the brief and how the project came about?
January Moon is a line of contemporary teething jewellery from artist/designer Jenny Luckett.
With the birth of her son, Jenny found she could no longer wear her favorite pieces of jewellery
and set out to create something that could satisfy both mama and baby's discerning tastes.
Where most teething jewellery can feel like a child's toy, her jewellery was modern and beautiful,
inspired by art and function. Jenny came to Perky Bros to create an identity and packaging
to reflect the spirit and aesthetic of the brand.

Walk us through the design process that you went through for this project?

We always start with a discovery session with the client to understand the history, needs and values of the brand they've crafted. We craft a creative brief, do extensive competitive research and create moodboards to direct the visuals of the brand concepts. We then explore stories and metaphors that can bring the brand to life. For January Moon, the brand name is inspired by the snowy winter night her son was born. We were inspired by the phases of the moon to provide both visual metaphor and a representation of the phases mother and baby experience together during this period.

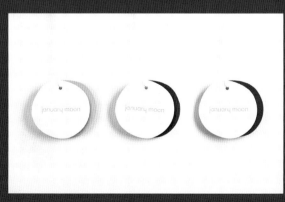

Where did the inspiration for the patterns come from?

The pattern shapes were inspired by the phases of the moon – abstractions of full, half and slivers are used in organic compositions to feel modern with a sense of play. They were cut by hand with coloured paper in reference to the modern artwork work of Matisse, as well as the imperfectness of a child's handiwork. The palette features primary colours as a reference to the playfulness of childhood and mid-century art, bright in contrast when placed on the snowy white of the packaging and printed materials.

How can effective design enhance a client's brand identity?

Effective identity design is the greatest tool to communicate a brand's personality. When done right, it sets the brand apart from the competition, creates memorable connections and adds value to the brand as a whole.

Were there any technical issues in creating the packaging?

Based on the client's budget, we needed be smart with how it was created. We needed to find a way to make off the shelf boxes unique and high-end to reflect the quality of the jewellery. Creating multiple pattern compositions on the belly bands allowed the packaging to be more unique and artful. Diecut tags and screenprinting added more customisation and something truly unique.

Share one lesson that you learned while developing the finished product.

Production and cost mandatories brought multiple lessons for how to best push our resources. We worked with our printers and vendors to print multiple designs on larger parent sheets to get as many pieces as possible. This added to the overall value and ensured the brand felt more developed and polished.

Bombay Electric Multibrand clothing store
Michael Thorsby michaelthorsby.com

Second Choice Clothing & jewellery
Noeeko noeeko.com

Kindo

~~~~~~~~~~~~~~~~~~~~~~~~~~~~~~~~~~~~~~~

Anagrama
anagrama.com

Kindo's colour palette attempts to reflect a child's personality, using a wide range of pastel and neon colours.

Kindo is an exclusive boutique for kids' clothing and accessories in Mexico and offers a wide selection of trendsetting and original clothing items for children.

The brand, which has been created by Anagrama, is inspired by a didactic bead maze, made up of geometric shapes, which feature heavily on the packaging. Kindo's colour palette attempts to reflect a child's personality, using a wide range of pastel and neon colours. The icon represents the mix of the classic and the new that make up the brand and gives the packaging a contemporary, fun and friendly aesthetic.

Photo Caroga Foto / carogafoto.com

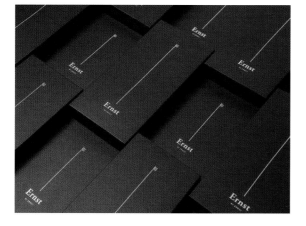

Barboza

~~~~~~

Maksim Arbuzov
maksimarbuzov.com

Made from a combination of sustainable materials, the box is completely recyclable.

Barboza, a company selling premium gym and
fitness apparel online, has always used
carbon-neutral DHL GoGreen shipping.
Now this approach is complemented
by the use of sustainable cardboard
in its packaging. Barboza is currently
going through the process of gradually
banishing all the PVC-based materials
within its packaging and replacing it
with sustainable packaging.
Made from a combination of sustainable
materials, the box, designed by Maksim
Arbuzov, is completely recyclable.
The print is made with water-based paint
and the adhesive is a glue-based on potato
starch. The vegetable-based packaging
provides not only a health-friendly
packaging alternative to PVC bags,
but also ensures sustainable disposal
as wastepaper.

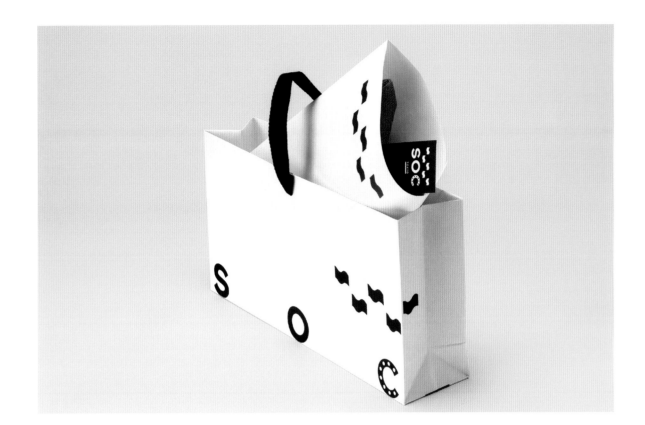

SOC TOKYO Socks
Keiko Akatsuka & Associates keikored.tv

cottonii Handkerchiefs
FROM GRAPHIC fromgraphic.jp

Mani Shoes
Larssen & Amaral larssenamaral.no

Eat My Shorts Clothing brand
Black Canvas helloblackcanvas.com

Addition Adelaide Tokyo Fashion & concept store
Homework homework.dk

Le Ciel Bleu Japanese fashion brand
Homework homework.dk

Home

"Effective design contributes to the brand building effort and makes the message that the brand is communicating clearer."

Essen International

Mathias Dahlgren Edition
Essen International

Mathias Dahlgren Edition

Essen International
esseninternational.com

What was the brief for this project and how did the opportunity come about?
Grand Hotel Stockholm, retailer Dafra and chef Mathias Dahlgren had developed a modern, high-quality set of kitchen appliances. They asked us to create a packaging solution that could go hand-in-hand with their premium products. The brief was quite open, except for the technical limitations.

Dow did the collaborative relationship with Matthias work?

Our process started with some key insights that we gained through retail visits, analysis of the national and international competition and benchmarks. We identified a very dark impression overall, there was an overload of information and more or less all of the competitors used product images on their packaging. Obviously, with that as a foundation, we saw an opportunity to create something unique with great standout. We then visited Mathias' restaurant for inspiration, and observed how the kitchen works. Mathias was also involved in key decision making stages and gave us opinions on the overall direction.

What were the technical issues in creating the packaging?

The most challenging part would be that the structure and shape of the packaging is predefined, but it seems that our minimal approach managed to get around that limitation pretty well.

How is a client's brand identity enhanced by effective design?

A brand identity is built by aligned expression and behavior throughout various touch points. Effective design contributes to the brand building effort and makes the message that the brand is communicating clearer. In our case, Mathias is a strong brand, as a superstar chef here in Sweden, so our packaging design solution amplifies that fact.

What information did you feel was necessary to include and what did you intentionally leave off?

I think the most important information on a package is the product names, in this case, the sizes of the products as well. That's why we had them on four sides of the box, while the rest of the information was placed on the two short sides. We did so because of the overall concept and in general, our functional design approach. Minimal design expression usually signals quality, for example, if you look at Apple's packaging. So too does the craftsmanship and details of the printing, where we used a very subtle silver colour for the grey to convey quality.

What was one of the biggest goals you set out to achieve and how did you accomplish it?

I think for us, every project is about finding the best design solution for whatever problems our clients face. In this case, we were aiming to help Mathias successfully launch his first kitchen products. On a design level, we were trying to create the best possible translation of Mathias' cooking philosophy. We accomplished it by turning the natural ingredients in his cooking in to a basic graphic language of shapes and letters.

Modern

~~~~~~

COLLINS
wearecollins.com

The shared solution celebrates a deep respect for American modernism.

Target partnered with design and architecture publication Dwell and co-designers Chris Deam and Nick Dine, to develop a new home collection titled 'Modern by Dwell Magazine'. The line has been custom-designed for style seekers who want to create a relaxing residence with a modern aesthetic, but believe that obtaining this look means having to sacrifice comfort.

Target engaged COLLINS to help create the brand to be applied to packaging, communications and retail environments. To bring the spirit behind the collection to life, Target & COLLINS drew inspiration from the same modernist ethos that Chris Deam and Nick Dine used to approach the product design.

The original ambition of modernist design was democratic – the goal was to make great design affordable for everyone. This new line by Target and Dwell Magazine speaks to that nascent intention of modernist design – it is the kind of design that's within reach for everybody. The shared solution celebrates a deep respect for American modernism, while organising all of the different elements in an uplifting manner.

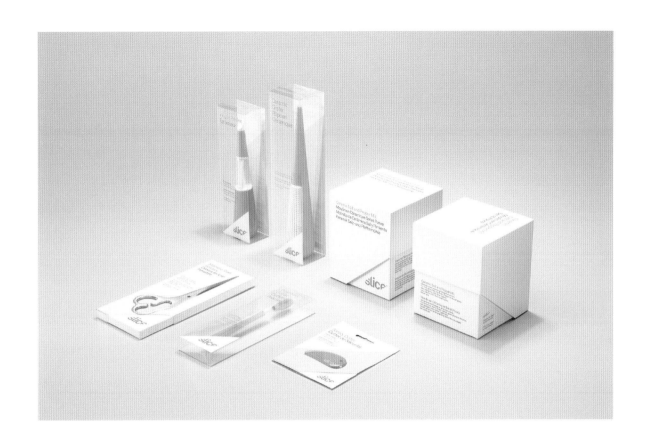

Slice Homeware
Manual manualcreative.com

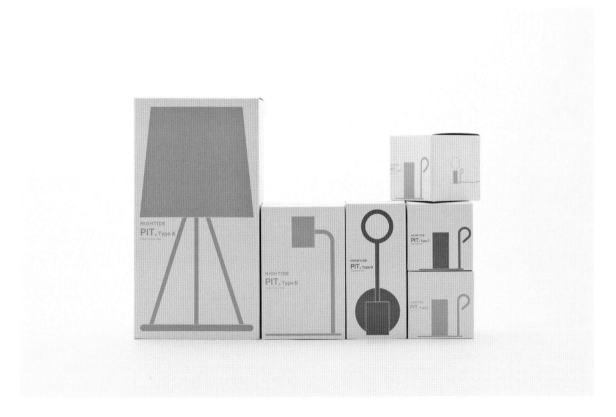

Pit Lighting
Doogdesign. en.doogdesign.jp

HOME

Wink Limited Edition Containers Home decor
Wink wink-mpls.com

Nostalgi Hat rack for Essem Design
Bedow bedow.se

HOME

Bute Fabrics sample box
Graphical House graphicalhouse.com

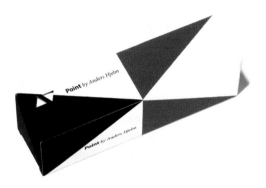

Point Wall hook for Essem Design
Bedow bedow.se

Moomin Shop Moomin Shop products
Bond Creative Agency bond-agency.com

D-MOD Lighting collection
talc design studio talcdesignstudio.com

Nest Consumer technology
Manual manualcreative.com

Golorful Headphone
Frame inc. frame-d.jp

Golorful
cloth pattern headphone

Freewheel

~~~~~~

COLLINS
wearecollins.com

The energetic lines on the packaging express the idea of, 'a free and strong WiFi signal that is available almost everywhere'.

Freewheel is a mobile phone powered by a dedicated WiFi network with over one million hotspots. The phone was created so customers could have a more economical choice to the expensive data overages and hidden fees of large cellular companies. COLLINS created the system, digital product language and packaging for the brand. The energetic lines on the packaging express the idea of, 'a free and strong WiFi signal that is available almost everywhere'.

Finchtail Tablet Stand Tablet/phone stand
Believe in® believein.net

uBear High-end mobile phone, tablet & laptop accessories
Hype Type Studio hypetype.studio

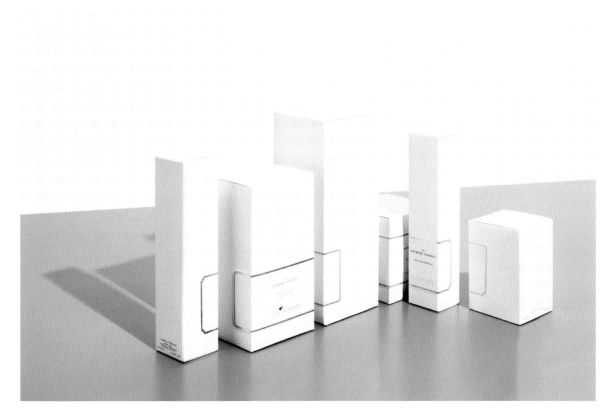

Julie Fagerholt/Heartmade – Fragrance Fragrance line for the home including room spray, diffuser & scented candle
Homework homework.dk

Mask Bathroom spray
makebardo makebardo.com

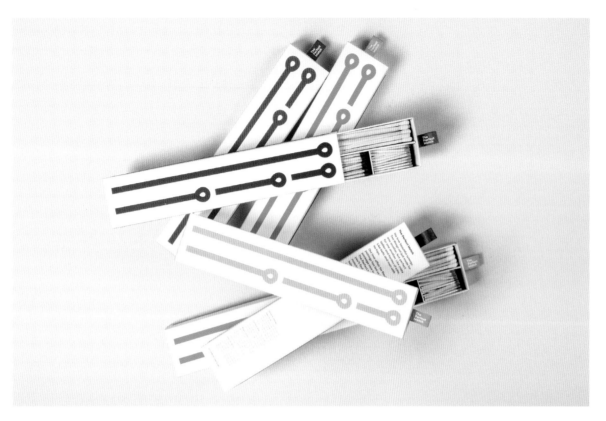

The Perfect Match Box of matches, originally produced as a holiday gift
to Leo Burnett's clients
Leo Burnett Design, Toronto leoburnettdesign.ca

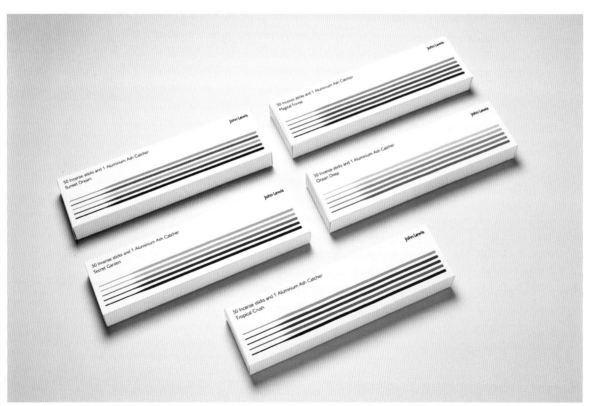

John Lewis, Incense Packaging Incense
Charlie Smith Design charliesmithdesign.com

Candlefish Matchbox design for a candle company
Fuzzco fuzzco.com

Klar Homeware
Bielke&Yang bielkeyang.com **Photo** Jonas Grytemark

Spongie Body sponges
Luminous Design Group luminous.gr

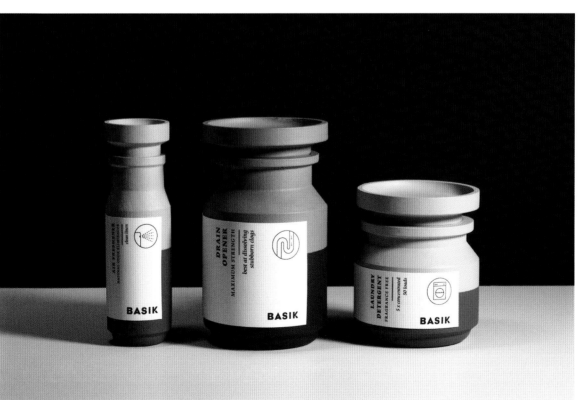

Clean The Ocean Biodegradable cleaning agent KOREFE. Kolle Rebbe Form und Entwicklung korefe.de

BASIK Personal hygiene & household goods HELLSTEN hellsten.co

NaturePaint Eco-friendly paint
B&B studio ltd bandb-studio.co.uk

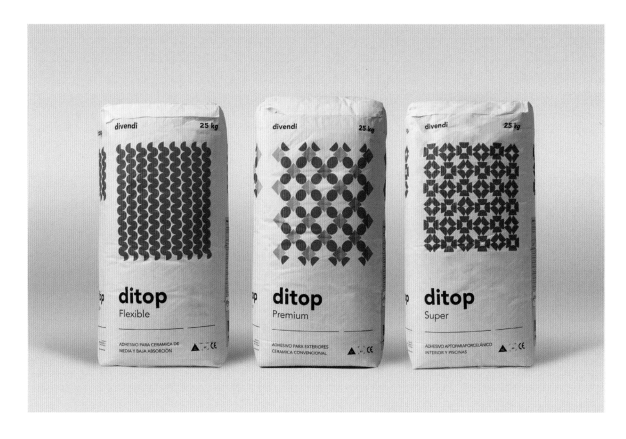

Ditop Cement
Rubio & del Amo rubioydelamo.com

Bricos

Anagrama
anagrama.com

In order to develop the branding strategy, Anagrama first executed a deep brand diagnostic, which resulted in a solution that helped the company convey their values.

Bricos had a very clear goal, 'to stop being your typical hardware shop and become a construction material supplier of high esteem, that could compete on an international stage'.

In order to develop the branding strategy, Anagrama first executed a deep brand diagnostic, which resulted in a solution that helped the company convey their values such as service, honesty, responsibility, experience and kindness, key to the company's success throughout the years and to install a sense of pride in its workforce.

Anagrama achieved this by creating a timeless brand with a unique icon unlike any of its competitors, by utilising a clean typographic language and a pattern that can be easily applied to any object.

Photo Caroga Foto / carogafoto.com

Index

COUNTER-PRINT PACKAGING